COLD WAR

By Bob Fowke
(with drawings by the same)

Dedicated to the squirrels of Central Park - they
couldn't keep secrets.

Hodder
Childr
Boo

a division of Hodder

D0582886

Text and illustrations, copyright © Bob Fowke 2001

The right of Bob Fowke to be identified as the author of the work has been asserted by him in accordance with the Copyright, Designs and Patents Act 1988.

Produced by Fowke & Co. for Hodder Children's Books

Cover photo: John Kennedy and Nikita Khrushchev. Picture supplied by the John F. Kennedy Library.

Published by Hodder Children's Books 2001

0340 788070

10 9 8 7 6 5 4 3 2 1

Hodder Children's Books,
a Division of Hodder Headline Limited
338 Euston Road
London NW1 3BH

Printed and bound by the Guernsey Press Co. Ltd., Channel Islands
A Catalogue record for this book is available from the British Library

CONTENTS

Watch out for the *Sign of the Foot*! Whenever you see this sign in the book it means there are some more details at the *FOOT* of the page. Like here.

NIGHTMARE!

ARE YOU SLEEPING SOUNDLY?

It's October 1962. You're asleep in your bed. You don't know about international politics and you don't care. It's hot and you're dreaming of a nice, cold ice lolly. Maybe, if you've been reading the newspapers, your ice lolly may look a bit like a nuclear missile, but apart from that you're sleeping soundly.

Sleep soundly while you can - because you're about to have a nightmare.
This nightmare is going to be worse than any nightmare you've ever had before: right now while you're sleeping, President John F. Kennedy of the USA is about to open the fridge door ...

MIND THE FRIDGE, JOHN!

In your nightmare, President John Kennedy of the USA and the Russian leader Nikita Khrushchev ✒ are going to let the Cold War out of the fridge. The Cold War is going to get hot!

Third World War

Pronounced 'Croosh-chov'.

BACK TO REALITY

'Cold War' is the name given to the long dispute between America and her allies on one side and Russia and her allies on the other side, which started in 1945 at the end of the Second World War and ended around 1990. It's called 'cold' because it never turned into a 'hot' war with real weapons - except round the edges.

But in October 1962, the nightmare very nearly became reality - the Cold War very nearly went *hot*. October was the month of the Cuban Missile Crisis, and in that month, the two sides came within a cat's whisker of total disaster. For a few incredibly dangerous days, America and Russia almost bombed each other, and the rest of us, into nuclear oblivion. Luckily for us, both John Kennedy and the Russian leader Nikita Khrushchev backed off at the last minute.

They kept the fridge door closed - just.

Allies are friendly countries who agree to defend each other in times of war.

NUKE EM!

This is my version of the god of nuclear terror.
What would *your* version be like?

ON YOUR MARX

HOW IT ALL BEGAN
COLD WAR BOARS

The Cold War was a struggle between two systems 🐾.
On one side were capitalist countries led by America.
On the other side were communist countries, led by
Russia.

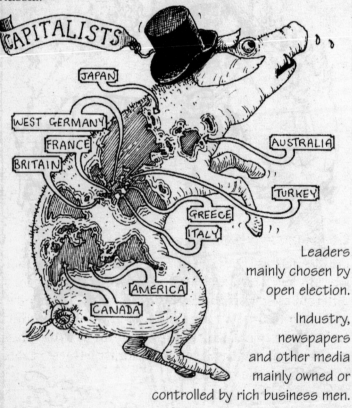

Leaders
mainly chosen by
open election.

Industry,
newspapers
and other media
mainly owned or
controlled by rich business men.

 System here means how a country is organised: politics, business,
culture - everything.

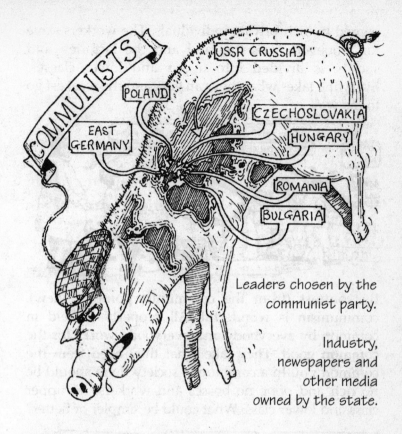

COMMUNISTS

POLAND

EAST GERMANY

USSR (RUSSIA)

CZECHOSLOVAKIA

HUNGARY

ROMANIA

BULGARIA

Leaders chosen by the communist party.

Industry, newspapers and other media owned by the state.

Communism is wonderful

On the face of it, it's hard to understand why there was any need for a Cold War. The two systems were as different as stale cabbage and fresh lettuce. Capitalism was old and tired by the time Russia went communist early in the twentieth century. Why didn't the whole world plump for the fresh communist lettuce as soon as it came on the menu?

After all (from the communist point of view), capitalism is dreadful. Under capitalism the 'means of production' (factories, mines, farms etc.) are mostly owned by rich private individuals. The workers slave for whoever owns the land and the factories, and society is divided into upper and lower classes. Everyone takes what they can get - and the weakest go to the wall.

By contrast (from the communist point of view), communism is wonderful. All property is held in common by everybody and everybody works for the common good. They take what they need from the common pot. In a communist society there should be no rich and poor, no bosses and workers, no upper class and lower class. What could be simpler or better?

That's communism in theory; reality is more complicated. If communism is to work properly, nobody should be lazy or greedy or ambitious for power. If some people are *naturally* lazy, greedy and ambitious, then other people are going to end up working a lot harder than others - just as they do under capitalism. Communists get round this by arguing that laziness, greed and ambition are caused by the unfair and unequal society in which we all live. Give us a nice, happy, equal world to live in, they say, and we'll *all* be hard-working and happy.

How it all began

Modern communism was started by a German called Karl Marx who came to live in London in 1847. At that time many people, Marx among them, were horrified by the conditions endured by workers in the new, capitalist factories of the Industrial Revolution, which had started in England in the eighteenth century. So when he first arrived in London, Marx joined a group of exiled German craftsmen who wanted to change things. They called themselves the 'League of the Just'. He wrote a manifesto  for them and called it the *Communist Manifesto*. Shortly after, the group changed their name to the 'Communist League'.

 A manifesto is a wish list of what a political party or group would like to do and why, if they achieve power.

In the *Communist Manifesto* Marx spelled out his theory of why the world was divided into rich and poor and how things would change for the better. His theory stated that all human societies are run for the benefit of their ruling class and that human history is driven by the struggles between classes – in other words: what *class* you belong to is more important than what *country* you come from.

'Marxism', as his theory became known, was a gospel of hope. No wonder it appealed to so many people. According to Marx, with each new revolution in technology a new ruling class comes to power. Once there were hunters ruled by tribal elders, then agriculture came along and there were kings. Then industry came along and the world was ruled by capitalists. That stage too would pass and then, sure as eggs is eggs (by Marx's calculation), it would be the workers' turn to rule.

INTERNATIONAL ANTICS

As far as communists were concerned, the Cold War of 1945-90 was just part of a struggle which started long ago when communism started. The struggle was international from the very beginning. As Marx put it in the *Communist Manifesto*:

> *The proletarians* *have nothing to lose but their chains. They have a world to win. Working men of all countries unite!*

The first 'International Working Men's Association', which became known as the 'First International', was set up in London in 1864 with Marx as its leading member (not all the other members were communists). Its job was to work for a working class revolution. Marx himself became internationally famous after a revolution in Paris in 1871, called the 'Paris Commune'. This seemed to bear out many of his theories because, among other things, it was an uprising of the Parisian working class.

By *proletarians* he meant working class people.

Unfortunately for the communists, the Paris Commune was crushed within a year and the communist movement went into retreat along with other revolutionary movements. Marx's close friend Friedrich Engels persuaded the First International to move its headquarters to New York, out of harm's way, fearing that he and Marx were about to lose control over it. Once in New York, it soon withered and died (1876).

Marx died eight years later. At the time of his burial in Highgate cemetery, London, the communist revolution seemed as far away as ever.

UNCLE JOE ★

A NIGHTMARE IN THE MAKING

THE TOUGHEST ANIMAL IN THE ZOO

After the defeat of the Paris Commune in 1871, the struggle for communism moved east, to a vast, cold land ruled by a savage government - to Russia.

If anywhere was ripe for revolution it was Russia in the late nineteenth century. Russian workers were treated like dogs. Any attempt to change things was viciously stamped on by the government. Revolutionaries were shot, exiled and imprisoned. Russian communists had to be men and women of iron simply in order to survive. It's hardly surprising that Russian communism grew up to be the toughest animal in the zoo ...

THE REVOLUTION ARRIVES

In 1902, a Russian communist called Vladimir Illyich Lenin wrote a short book called *What is to be Done?* At that time the Russian workers were weak because there weren't many of them - Russia had only just started to industrialise. Lenin argued that Russian communists should turn themselves into a small band of disciplined, professional revolutionaries (the 'Vanguard of the Proletariat') who would lead the workers to power.

In 1903, a small majority of the Russian revolutionary movement decided to follow Lenin's ideas. They became known as the *Bolsheviki* - 'the Majority'.

In February 1917 in the depths of the bitter Russian winter, the Russian ruler Czar Nicholas II was overthrown in a revolution led by angry soldiers and sailors. They were fed up with the horrors of World War I (1914-18). A new, revolutionary government was set up - but as yet the Bolsheviks weren't in control.

In Moscow and St Petersburg the workers, soldiers and sailors formed themselves into 'soviets ' and elected their own leaders to run things. The Bolsheviks put themselves at the head of these soviets wherever possible.

In October the Bolsheviks, led by Lenin, seized power in an armed coup . From now on, they claimed, the country would be run by the soviets of workers and peasants. In actual fact it was to be run by the Bolsheviks. The Czar and his family were shot in cold blood.

In the emergency which followed, the Soviet government abolished money, took all Russian industries away from their private owners, made work compulsory and forced the peasants to exchange their food for next to nothing. This terrible period was called 'War Communism'.

 Soviet is Russian for 'council'.

 Coup here means a sudden, violent change of government.

Russia broke down in turmoil. There was mass starvation and civil war. Britain, America and France sent help to the anti-Bolshevik forces. Winston Churchill said they should 'throttle infant Bolshevism in the cradle'. As far as Russian communists are concerned, this is when the Cold War really started.

In order to cling onto power the Bolsheviks started a campaign of terror, shooting many of their enemies.

The Bolsheviks hung onto power. Thanks to Lenin and the terror, communism had got its first toe-hold in the world - if you could call it communism.

Who gobbles who?

Communism had taken hold in Russia, but most of the rest of the world was still capitalist. The workers of the world were still in chains and the big, fat capitalist wolf would gobble the communists up if the communists didn't gobble the capitalists up first. As Lenin put it:

Ultimately one or the other must conquer.

In 1919 Lenin set up the Third International, otherwise known as the 'Comintern', to fight for world revolution. The Comintern was a very tough organisation: all the national parties from different countries which joined it had to obey its decisions. Since the Comintern was dominated by Lenin, this meant that the communist parties of the world became tools of the Bolsheviks - the Russian Communist Party.

International box

First International 1864-76
Second International 1889-c.1914
Third International (Comintern) 1919-43

 The Second International had been formed in 1889 but had never been controlled by communists.

21

MAN OF STEEL

The Russians had a tough time under the early Bolsheviks, but worse was to follow. Lenin died in 1924. His successor was a brutal tyrant called Stalin . Stalin was a bully with a pock-marked face and one arm shorter than the other. He came from Georgia in the south where he'd been brought up by a drunken father who beat him savagely - Stalin had learned early that might is right.

Stalin arranged for the murder or execution of all his rivals for power and tightened his grip on the young USSR - 'Union of Soviet Socialist Republics', or 'Soviet Union' - as Russia called itself from 1922. His terror extended to all the communist parties of the Comintern.

Stal is Russian for steel. A very rough translation of Stalin is 'Man of Steel'.

Stalin was a brute but he got things done. Starting in 1928, he built factories, roads and railways. In fact Russia is the only country to have industrialised itself without foreign investment apart from eighteenth-century Britain - and it was equally hard on the workers. Stalin was utterly ruthless. Up to *twenty-two million* people died from starvation, execution or just sheer, brutal hard work and suffering.

UNCLE JOE

By the 1930s, thanks to Lenin and then Stalin, the communist dream had turned into a communist nightmare. To help the communists keep control there were secret police everywhere. Children were encouraged to betray their parents to the authorities if their parents spoke out against the government, even when they were safe at home. Wives were encouraged to betray their husbands, and friends to betray each other. Russia had become one huge prison camp. Nobody was safe from the terror.

TAKE HIM- YOU'RE WELCOME!

Then the Second World War started and something odd happened. Nazi Germany invaded Russia and suddenly the Soviet Union and the capitalist countries of the west, Britain and later America in particular, found themselves on the same side - against the Germans . On the morning after the Nazi invasion, Stalin woke up to find that he had lots of capitalist friends whom he'd never known about. He was given the nickname 'Uncle Joe' by the western press.

Of course, it was wishful thinking on the part of the west. Uncle Joe was never the sort of uncle you would want to ask back for a cup of tea - as his victims could have explained, if anyone had asked them. But nobody did. Instead, communists in the west chose to believe that the Soviet Union was a paradise on Earth.

At the start of the war Stalin made a pact with the Nazis, and the Soviet Union gobbled up various small countries as its reward. But the Nazis were only playing for time until they were ready to turn on the USSR.

COUNT YOUR MARX

(Answers on page 122.)

**1 What group did Karl Marx join
when he first came to London?**

a The Manifesto Group
b The Communist Workers'
International Brotherhood of
Communist Workers
c The League of the Just

2 What is Marxism?

a A system for scoring good marks in class
b A political theory about classes
c A class of theories about exam marks
d A political theory about exams

3 What does Bolshevik mean?

a The majority
b The minority
c A bad-tempered Viking

**4 What might children do
in Stalin's Russia?**

a Go hungry
b Betray their parents
c Study business management
with a view to getting on in life

WHO DREW THE IRON CURTAIN?

THE COLD WAR BEGINS

A SACRIFICE ON THE ALTAR OF YALTA

While the Second World War was still going on, Stalin met up with Winston Churchill, the British Prime Minister, and Theodore Roosevelt, the American President. The big three wanted to discuss what they should do with Europe once they'd beaten the Germans.

They met in February 1945, at Yalta, a Russian holiday resort on the Black Sea, in the old Livadia Palace which had been built for poor Czar Nicholas II back in 1914. It was so crowded that sixteen American colonels had to share one room (and the bed bugs that came with it). At that time, Russians, British and Americans were all chums together - the feeling was that 'of a family' as Roosevelt put it.

SHOVE OVER!

At Yalta the British and Americans accepted that the huge army of the Soviet Union was bound to dominate the countries of eastern Europe, such as Poland and Hungary, once the war was over. In return for accepting this unpleasant but rather unavoidable fact, the British and Americans trusted, or rather *hoped*, that Stalin would allow free elections in the countries of eastern Europe.

GETTING COLDER

Three months after Yalta, the war in Europe ended. The Russians had fought their way into Germany from the east and the British, Americans and other Allies had done the same from the west. The two victorious forces ground to a halt facing each other in a long line which cut right across Germany and all the way down to the Mediterranean Sea.

And *that's* when the big freeze started - Stalin had no intention of letting capitalist armies into the Soviet patch. His idea was for a 'fortress Russia' surrounded by small states under his total control. The line between the two sides soon froze solid. With some adjustments, it became the border between communist and capitalist worlds for the next forty-five years - in fact, for the entire Cold War.

Of course, Stalin was no more interested in elections than a cat is interested in a cabbage. His communist secret police gradually began to arrest anyone who might stand up to them in eastern Europe. Before long, communists held all the real power in that part of the world.

THE IRON CURTAIN GETS PULLED

Meanwhile a new president took over in America. To start with, Harry Truman trusted the Russians as much as Roosevelt had done at Yalta. In June 1945 he wrote in his diary:

I'm not afraid of the Russians. They've always been our friends.

But by January 1946, having seen what Stalin and his secret police were up to in eastern Europe, Truman was singing a different tune:

There's only one language they understand - how many divisions have you? I'm tired of babying the Soviets.

Now a division is a group of army regiments. What Truman meant was that the Soviets only understood brute force. There was no point in being nice to them.

Tempers were rising. In March 1946, Winston Churchill went to visit Truman in America. He was due to give a speech at Fulton Missouri. (The two men shared a railway carriage and played poker all the way - Churchill won.) Churchill's speech at Fulton is usually thought to herald the start of the Cold War:

> ... *from Stettin in the Baltic to Trieste in the Adriatic, an iron curtain has descended across the continent ...*

TUNE NUMBER 1

By the time Churchill made his speech, the stage had already been set for the most terrifying aspect of the Cold War. Japan, Germany's most powerful ally, hadn't surrendered along with the Germans in May 1945. The Japanese fought every step of the way, from one Pacific island to another. The cost in human life was horrific. On Okinawa even the civilians chose to fight to the death.

The Americans decided to shock the Japanese into surrender. From late 1943, British and American scientists had been working on the top secret *Manhattan Project* to develop a nuclear bomb, and in 1945 they were ready. This terrifying new weapon was demonstrated to the world on 6 August when the

Americans dropped it on the Japanese city of Hiroshima. Three days later they dropped another one on the city of Nagasaki. Around 120,000 people died, with many more dying later from radiation sickness (see page 49).

President Truman was famous for pithy sayings:

If you can't stand the heat, get out of the kitchen.

By this he meant that it was the duty of leaders to take hard decisions and to cope with the pressure of life at the top, or they shouldn't be leaders. Nothing can have been harder than the decision to drop the bomb.

Looking back, it's not easy to understand why he didn't demonstrate its power to the Japanese in some other way before dropping it on their cities, perhaps by blowing up an uninhabited island. But those were times of war and, for better or for worse, the deed was done. When people looked out of their windows the day after Hiroshima, they realised that a new and more terrifying world had been born. If the Cold War was a soap opera, that was when the world first heard its theme tune:

nuclear terror.

Truman had another saying. He had it printed on a notice on his desk. It read:

The buck stops here .

Responsibility for dropping the first nuclear bomb on a live target is one buck most of us could do without.

 During poker games in the old Wild West, a buckhorn-handled knife was often placed on the table to mark who was dealer. If someone didn't want to deal, they 'passed the buck'.

TUNE NUMBER 2

The Russians were naturally terrified by the bomb in case the Americans used it against *them*. They set out to build one of their own as soon as possible. But in the meantime they were also very worried by something you would expect them to be happy about - the offer of lots of dollars in American aid. Poor Europe, both east and west, was on its knees after the devastation of the Second World War and the Americans had decided to throw money at it, 'Marshall Aid' as it was called after General Marshall who organised it. It was meant to put Europe back on its feet.

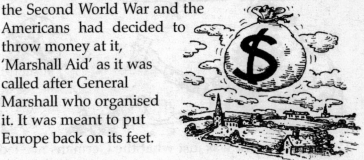

Actually, the Americans never really intended to lend money to the Russians. They made it clear that the Russians would have to ask for American permission over how the money would be spent - which they knew that Stalin would never agree to. Russia refused Marshall Aid.

So here was another theme tune for the Cold War soap opera:

The west was about to get a lot richer than the east.

AID AND BLOCKADE

When the war ended, conquered Germany was divided into four sectors each controlled by either

33

Russian, American, British or French troops. Marshall Aid flowed into the sectors controlled by the Americans, British and French but not into the Russian-controlled sector. The Americans, British and French also allowed their sectors of Berlin, the old German capital, to start using the new German currency - the deutschmark.

The deutschmark was just what the Germans needed to get their economy going again, so Stalin didn't like it. Like all Russians, he was terrified of Germany becoming strong again. He especially didn't want the deutschmark to be used in Berlin.

Although Berlin was divided between American, French, British and Russian control, it was actually deep inside the Russian-controlled sector of Germany, like a sort of island. It was linked to the west by a narrow corridor of land. Stalin decided to starve the western part of the city (the part which he didn't control) into surrender. He cut the land corridor to the west and started a blockade .

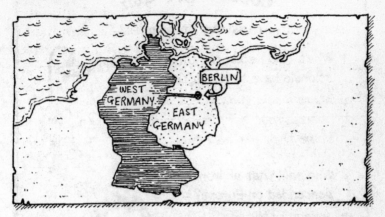

Between June 1948 and May 1949, West Berlin was supplied entirely by air from the west. Nearly 2.5 million tons of food and other supplies were flown into the city. There was no other way to beat the blockade.

In the meantime the Americans stationed nuclear bombers in Britain - within range of Russia - just in case. The Berlin Blockade was the first time the Cold War nearly went hot.

In a blockade, food and other supplies are not allowed into the place which is being blockaded.

COOLING OFF QUIZ

(Answers on page 122.)

1 What did sixteen United States colonels have to do at Yalta?

a Share a cold shower

b Share a room

c Share their sandwiches

2 Who said that an Iron Curtain had descended on Europe?

a Joseph Stalin

b Harry Truman

c Winston Churchill

3 Where did the buck stop?

a On Truman's desk

b In a railway carriage where Truman and Churchill were playing poker

c In a clearing in the forest

4 What was the Iron Curtain?

a An enormous curtain made out of iron which was drawn across the middle of Germany by heavy machinery

b A way of describing the division of Europe between communists and capitalists

COLD WAR COUNTDOWN - PART I

THE ROAD TO RUIN

FINGERS OFF THE TRIGGER!

The Cold War started in earnest after the Berlin Blockade. One year freezing, the next year just frosty, the temperature kept changing - but fingers were never far from nuclear buttons.

4 April 1949 - NATO. Led by America, the countries of the 'free world' as they called themselves, banded together in a massive defensive pact, the *North Atlantic Treaty Organisation*. At its largest in 1952, NATO stretched from the USA in the west to Turkey in the east, and from Canada in the north to Italy in the south. Most of the richest countries in the world were members. NATO drew up detailed plans for how the armed forces of the member countries would work together if the Soviets attacked.

14 July 1949 - First Soviet atom bomb. The USSR tested its first atom bomb four years after Hiroshima. Americans were shocked. Aggressive American senator McMahon suggested what America should do to Russia:

> ... *blow them off the face of the Earth* ... *we haven't much time.*

24 June 1950 - Start of the Korean War. The communists of North Korea under their President Kim Il Sung invaded South Korea in the first 'hot' conflict between communists and the 'free world'. The communists were thrown out of the south by the Americans and their allies, but when the Americans invaded the north, the communist Chinese joined in. Over 300,000 Chinese troops attacked at night to the sound of bugles. The Americans were thrown out of the north and the border between North and South Korea has been frozen in position ever since. Nearly two million men (mainly Koreans and Chinese) died in the Korean War.

5 March 1953 - Death of Stalin. Stalin was replaced by Nikita Khrushchev who was a lamb by comparison, although a lamb who did a lot of shouting. Khrushchev set out to remove the worst of Stalin's tyranny.

KHRUSHCHEV (1894-1971)

Nikita Khrushchev's grandfather was a serf  and his father was a miner. His first wife died of starvation in the 1920s. He was a bumptious, vulgar peasant of a man with a fat neck and a sense of humour. But clever. During the 1930s he was a keen supporter of Stalin and rose through the ranks of the Communist Party. He surprised everyone when he came to power and stopped the worst of Stalin's terror. In a speech in 1956 he denounced Stalin's:

... brutality, his abuse of power.

Khrushchev believed that communist and capitalist countries should compete peacefully to prove which system was best. During his time in power he was responsible for the Berlin Wall (page 41) and the Cuban Missile Crisis (page 43) but also for relaxation of Soviet oppression in eastern Europe. He lost power in 1964 but was allowed to live out his last seven years quietly.

Serfs are Russian slaves who go with the land, rather like Welsh sheep.

14 May 1955 - Warsaw Pact. Russia and her east European allies formed the *Warsaw Pact* in answer to NATO. This was because West Germany had been allowed to join NATO and the Russians were very cross about it. The countries of the Warsaw Pact agreed to defend each other if attacked.

3 November 1956 - Hungarian Uprising. At midnight, 250,000 Soviet troops attacked Budapest, the capital of communist Hungary. Led by a popular Prime Minister called Imre Nagy, Hungary had dared to ask the Russians to leave. 250,000 Hungarians were killed trying to resist the Soviet troops and Nagy himself was executed. Most communists in western countries were horrified. Many of them stopped believing in Soviet-style communism.

4 October 1957 - Sputnik  launched. The Russian *Sputnik* was the first man-made object ever to fly in space. The Americans were deeply shocked to discover that Russian technology was so advanced. As usual in the Cold War, they exaggerated. American political adviser George Reedy said:

> *... the race for control of the Universe has started.*

17 April 1961 - Bay of Pigs. In 1959 Cuban communists led by Fidel Castro took power in Cuba, a sunny Caribbean island right on America's doorstep. The Americans were horrified (again). In 1961, they supported a disastrous attempt to overthrow Castro's government - the Bay of Pigs invasion which was soundly defeated.

13 August 1961 - Berlin Wall. Communist troops began to build a wall right across the middle of Berlin, the divided German capital (see pages 33-35). The *Berlin Wall* was designed to stop East Germans fleeing to the rich western half of the city.

Sputnik is Russian for 'fellow traveller' or 'companion'.

When it was finished the Berlin Wall had 290 watchtowers, 105 km of trenches, 257 km of dog runs (for catching people) and 122 km of barbed wire fencing. It stayed in place for the next twenty-eight years.

1961 - Start of the Vietnam War. Throughout the 1960s America slowly increased its military support for the government of South Vietnam which was fighting a losing war against South Vietnamese communists. The South Vietnamese communists, or 'Vietcong' were supported by the separate communist state of North Vietnam. Before it lost the war in 1975, America had dropped more bombs on this one small country than had been dropped during the entire Second World War.

47,000 American soldiers were killed and well over a million Vietnamese.

JOHN F. KENNEDY (1917-63)

John Kennedy was handsome and young (for a president), and he had a beautiful wife called Jacqueline. During his time as president, the White House in Washington was known as Camelot, the mythical Palace of King Arthur, because the Kennedys had so many handsome and clever friends and advisers. Kennedy was president during the Cuban Missile Crisis and the building of the Berlin Wall. His great triumph was the Nuclear Test-Ban Treaty which he signed with Khrushchev and the British Prime Minister in 1963. They agreed to stop testing nuclear weapons both above ground and under water.

Kennedy was shot dead by an assassin in Dallas in 1963 during a presidential campaign.

22-28 October 1962 - Cuban Missile Crisis (where this book started). President Khrushchev decided to base Russian nuclear weapons on the island of Cuba, where they would be within easy striking distance of America. Russian ships steamed west with the missiles, and American President John Kennedy announced that American warships would stop them. The Russian ships only turned back at the last moment. If the Americans had fired on the Russians a nuclear war would definitely have started. As Dean Rusk, the American Secretary of State, put it when the confrontation was over:

We were eyeball to eyeball and the other fellow just blinked.

1963 - Détente. Both Americans and Russians (and everyone else) were scared silly by the Cuban Missile Crisis. Both realised how close to nuclear disaster they had come. A 'hotline' was installed so that the two presidents could talk to each other directly on the phone in times of crisis, and Kennedy made a speech about 'making the world safe for diversity', meaning that communists and capitalists must learn to live side by side. The idea of *détente*, meaning relaxation of tension, was born.

20 August 1968 - Prague Spring crushed. Soviet troops crushed a new, reforming government in communist Czechoslovakia, thus ending what became known as the *Prague Spring*. During the brief Prague Spring, writers were free to criticise communism.

Unfortunately Russian communists didn't like being criticised. At least Alexander Dubcek, the reformist Czech leader, wasn't shot. He ended up working in a timber yard.

February 1972 - Nixon visits China.
President Nixon of America visited communist China. China and Russia had become bitter enemies since they quarrelled in 1963 although both countries

were communist. After Nixon's visit to China, the Russians became frightened that America and China would gang up on them.

RICHARD MILHOUS NIXON (1913-94)

Richard Nixon was a fierce anticommunist in his younger days, working with top anticommunist Senator Joe McCarthy (see page 94). He was also the first and only president to resign from office. This was due to the Watergate Scandal, when his men were caught inside the headquarters of the opposition Democratic Party in the Watergate building in Washington. They were trying to steal files and to fit electronic 'bugs'.

45

26 May 1972 - SALT I. The first 'Strategic Arms Limitation Treaty' was signed in Moscow by President Richard Nixon and the Russian leader Leonid Brezhnev. The two sides agreed to limit their nuclear weapons. They also agreed to the building of a Pepsi-Cola factory in Russia.

Perhaps *détente* was beginning to work.

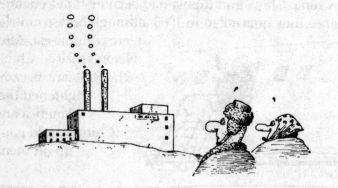

MEGA DEATH

ALL ABOUT NUCLEAR WEAPONS

THINKING IN MILLIONS

By the time *détente* got under way in the early 1970s, the two sides in the Cold War had learned to live with the idea of nuclear terror. They were like two tigers with razor-sharp teeth and claws who snarl and bristle but never actually pounce - because if they do, they'll rip each other to shreds. NATO and the Warsaw Pact each had enough nuclear weapons to blast the other back to the stone age. It was estimated that in the event of all-out nuclear war up to 66 million would die in the USA and up to 77 million in the USSR. Europe would be utterly flattened. *90% of the population of Britain could expect to die.*

In terms of power, nuclear weapons are as different to other weapons as an elephant is to a mouse. Their power is calculated in kilotons and megatons. Each kiloton is equal to a thousand tons of the high explosive TNT (trinitrotoluene) and each megaton is equal to a *million tons* of TNT. If you consider that during the Second World War the US Eighth Airforce dropped 700 kilotons of bombs in total, and that some modern nuclear bombers can carry two nuclear bombs of *ten megatons each* (twenty-eight times as much in total in one plane), you can see the difference. The largest nuclear blast ever was a test explosion by the USSR on 30 October 1961. It had a force of *fifty-seven megatons*.

BLAST IT - ALL ABOUT NUCLEAR EXPLOSIONS

If the Cold War had gone hot, the first thing for most of us would have been a blinding flash - literally blinding. This is the first sign of a nuclear explosion. Nuclear flash can burn out the retina of the eye, especially at night when the pupil is dilated to allow in as much light as possible.

Next would come heat. The heat at the centre of a nuclear explosion is as hot as the heat at the centre of the Sun. It travels outwards at 300 million metres per second and vaporises most things, including people, within 5 km of the centre of the explosion ('ground zero' as it's called). Further out, fires spring up all over the place fuelled by a fierce wind and causing a fire-storm.

Then would come the roar of the pressure wave. The pressure wave travels outward through the air and through the earth below as well. Even big buildings crumple like card houses.

Finally, if the flash, the heat and the pressure wave haven't done for us, there's still nuclear radiation. Deaths from radiation sickness continued for years after the bombs were dropped on Hiroshima and Nagasaki.

SPLITTING UP

There are two main types of nuclear bomb: the *atom bomb* (A-bomb) and the *hydrogen bomb* (H-bomb). In both cases the explosion is caused by a nuclear 'chain reaction'.

In an A-bomb the explosion is the result of *nuclear fission* (splitting or breaking apart). An ordinary chemical explosion starts the process by rapidly compressing a radioactive core of either uranium-235 or plutonium-239.

'Slow' neutrons in the radioactive core crash into the now densely-packed nucleii of the atoms of the core and split them apart.

The process feeds on itself: the splitting releases further neutrons which split open further nucleii and so on - a 'chain reaction' in other words.

Each time a nucleus splits it releases energy - and since the whole thing takes place in fractions of a second, enough energy is released to destroy whole cities.

Neutrons are subatomic particles. They are present in the nucleus (see below) of all atoms except hydrogen atoms.

Every atom has a *nucleus* (plural *nucleii*) - a small dense centre.

There is however a limit to the size of A-bombs. If the core of uranium or plutonium is too large it will have so many nucleii inside it that 'slow' neutrons are sure to bump into some of them and split them open without any help from outside - thus starting a chain reaction when you don't necessarily want one. The size at which this happens is called 'critical mass'.

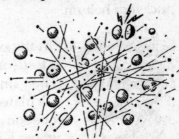

In fact, another way to explode an A-bomb is by suddenly joining two pieces of uranium or plutonium so that together they exceed critical mass.

AND GETTING TOGETHER

When it comes to *hydrogen bombs* there is no critical mass to limit the size of the explosion. Theoretically it would be quite possible to build a doomsday H-bomb which could destroy the entire world in a single explosion - although that would be rather pointless from the point of view of the people setting it off. One average-sized H-bomb can destroy a large city.

H-bombs work by *nuclear fusion* (joining together) of the light atomic nucleii of hydrogen to form heavier nucleii of helium.

In the process of fusion some mass is lost - or rather, it turns into energy. The amount of energy can be calculated using the famous equation of Albert Einstein, $E=mc2$, where E is energy, m is mass and c is the speed of light.

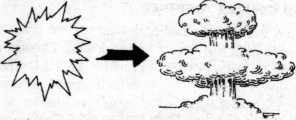

Einstein's equation means that the energy released is equal to the *mass which is lost* times the *speed of light* *squared* (the speed of light multiplied by itself) - which is one heck of a lot of energy and why hydrogen bombs are so powerful.

Nuclear fusion will only take place at very high temperatures (several million degrees) so H-bombs are called 'thermo-nuclear bombs'. (*Therme* is Greek for heat.) The heat is created by a small atomic explosion which triggers the thermo-nuclear explosion.

The speed of light is 299,792.458 kilometres per second (186,291 miles per second).

NUCLEAR FUN QUIZ

(Answers on page 122.)

1 In the event of a nuclear war, what percentage of the population of Great Britain could expect to die?

a 10%
b 50%
c 90%
d Everyone

2 How many kilotons in a megaton?

a Twenty
b A thousand
c A million

3 What is critical mass?

a An unfriendly audience at a concert
b The mass of hydrogen needed to start a chain reaction
c The mass of a lump of plutonium or uranium at which a chain reaction starts of its own accord

4 What's the first thing that would hurt you if you were close to a nuclear explosion?

a The pressure wave
b Nuclear flash
c Nuclear radiation

MADness!

At the cold heart of the Cold War lay *mutual terror*: the knowledge that the attackers would be utterly destroyed - even if they won. This was known as MAD, 'Mutual Assured Destruction', and it's what kept the peace for nearly fifty years, if that doesn't sound like a contradiction. Khrushchev put it well at the time of the Cuban Missile Crisis. President Kennedy reminded him that the USA had 4,000 nuclear warheads aimed at the USSR, enough to wipe out the Russians several times over, whereas the USSR only had enough warheads to wipe America out once. Khrushchev replied:

Once is quite enough.

Looking back, it's terrifying to realise how close the world came to disaster at that time. Khrushchev and Kennedy held back because, actually, they weren't mad. But it would be hard to say the same thing about some of the Russian and American generals who advised them. During the Cuban Missile Crisis Khrushchev once asked his generals if they understood that by standing up to the Americans 500 million human beings might die. As he recorded, the generals:

... looked at me as if I was out of my mind or, what was worse, a traitor ...

Back in America, President Eisenhower had claimed that the A-bomb should be used 'exactly as we would use a bullet or anything else'. As for the appalling General Powers, once head of the American Strategic Air Command, he once shouted:

Restraint?… The whole idea is to kill the bastards. At the end of the war, if there are two Americans and one Russian, we win …

And if *that* isn't bloodthirsty enough for you - Mao Tse-tung, Chairman of the Chinese Communist Party, once told Nehru, the Indian Prime Minister, that it might be no bad thing if half the world's population died in a nuclear war - so long as imperialism was defeated.

SO?

 Communists often called their capitalist enemies 'imperialists'. The idea being that they were trying to turn the whole world into their empire.

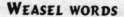

WEASEL WORDS

The reality of nuclear war was so horrific that the men who planned for it used special words to make it sound less awful.

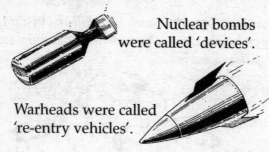

Nuclear bombs were called 'devices'.

Warheads were called 're-entry vehicles'.

The enemy's armed forces were called 'counter-force targets'.

Cities and factories were called 'counter-value targets'.

GETTING THERE

America and Russia are a long way away from each other. There are only two ways to deliver nuclear bombs to their targets over such a distance: either long range bombers or missiles with the bomb in the 'warhead'. Until the late 1950s, high-flying bombers could fly reasonably safely because fighter planes couldn't fly high enough to stop them .

But as defences got better both sides turned to missiles to deliver their bombs. Missiles are faster and harder to shoot down. The biggest missiles are called ICBMs, Intercontinental Ballistic Missiles. Fired upwards in a huge curve, at the high point of their flight they are outside the Earth's atmosphere. They have a range of more than 3,500 miles, often as much as 8,000 miles. When they re-enter the atmosphere, having shed most of the fuel which has powered them, the warhead with its guidance and defence systems plunges down towards its hapless target.

In the 1970s the Americans went one further. They invented MIRVs - Multiple Independently-Targetable Re-entry Vehicles. In this system each missile carries a

---

The best known of the American long range bombers, the B-52 designed in the 1940s, is still in use today.

number of warheads. On approaching their destination they split off from each other like a giant firework display, then each warhead heads for its own pre-selected target.

FIRST STRIKE

The nuclear game was a hair-trigger game. The flight time of missiles between the USA and the USSR is only around thirty-five minutes. Even with advanced early warning systems such as special satellites which detect the heat of missiles taking off, there was only eight minutes to react to an enemy attack and to launch defensive missiles before the enemy missiles hit home. React too late and you would be blasted to rubble - react too early (or wrongly) - and it would be you who started the war.

DON'T PRESS THAT BUTTON! THEY'RE JUST MIGRATING OSTRICHES.

The big fear was that the other side might launch a sudden attack and knock out all your weapons before there was any chance to fight back. Such an attack was called 'first strike'. If either side ever thought they could get away with a first strike, then there would be no threat of MAD. So both sides had to make sure that however hard the other side attacked, enough weapons would survive to strike back, known as 'second strike'. The threat of MADness was vital to both sides.

The missiles which would deliver the first and second strikes were kept ready to fire in special 'hardened' shelters called silos. Silos were best placed in 'springy' ground to help absorb the shock of attack. Often they were arranged in 'multiple protective structures': a single missile would be moved around a railway track at night between over twenty possible silos, so the other side would never know which one it was in.

Another scheme was to place up to a hundred missiles in 'super-hardened silos' in the hope that some would survive.

'Deep basing' was an American scheme. The missiles and the crews to fire them were to be lodged in tunnels up to 915 metres underground. The idea was that at the end of a nuclear 'exchange' the crews would dig their way to the surface with special digging machines and then fire off their weapons to ensure that MAD actually happened if the crunch came. The idea never came off because it was impossible to find earth soft enough to dig through but hard enough to withstand a direct nuclear hit.

TWENTY YEARS LATER...

WHEN THEY SAID 'SPECIAL DIGGING MACHINE', I THOUGHT THEY MEANT SOMETHING ELSE!

To counter the silos, special missiles were developed which could bore through to their targets. Pershing II, an American missile, could drive through most types of soil to a depth of about 30 metres before exploding.

SUBS

Perhaps the most dangerous launch pad for missiles was (and is) the nuclear submarine. Even during the

Second World War the Germans had designed an underwater barge with missile launchers which was to be pulled by submarine to the American coast.

The good thing about a submarine is that it's almost impossible for an enemy to track its movements through the vastness of the world's oceans. It's excellent for a first strike because it can move up close before launching its missiles thus reducing the warning time for the enemy. And it's good for a second strike because it can lurk underwater while nuclear hell is let loose on the surface, only surfacing later.

A VERY BIG TUB

The largest nuclear submarine ever was built by the Russians in 1977. It was designed to lie on the seabed beneath the arctic ice cap for up to a year at a time. One reason for its size was to stop the crew going barmy with boredom. It had a swimming pool and saunas where they could pass the time.

I'M NOT LOOKING FORWARD TO THE HOLIDAY.

SPACE RACE

OTHER USES FOR MISSILES

During the Cold War it was vitally important for both sides to *seem* to be winning: in sport, in wealth, in weapons - in space. If communism seemed to be winning then more people would want to go communist, and vice versa for capitalism. That was why the nuclear arms race led to the Space Race - both races used missile technology but the Space Race was a lot more fun and a lot less dangerous, except possibly for the astronauts.

SPUTNIKS AND PHUTNIKS

On 4 October 1957, a massive Soviet Intercontinental Ballistic Missile took off from Kazakhstan in the southern USSR. This ICBM wasn't aimed at America and it didn't carry a nuclear warhead. It carried a *Sputnik* ◄. The massive power of the missile punched right through Earth's gravity and launched the Sputnik into orbit ◄. It was the first ever satellite to orbit the Earth.

Sputnik became the name for a whole series of Soviet satellites.

Orbit means here: to circle the Earth high enough not to be pulled back to the surface by gravity and low enough not to drift away for ever.

The Americans were *PEEP* *PEEP* horrified. Safe in its orbit, Sputnik I flew four times across their continent, making an *PEEP* irritating beeping noise all the while, *PEEP* and there was nothing the Americans could do to stop it. Somehow those pesky communists had developed more advanced technology than America. How dare they? To rub salt in the wound, a month later the Russians launched another and much larger Sputnik. Sputnik II carried a husky dog called Laika. Sadly Laika died when her oxygen ran out.

In public President Eisenhower dismissed Sputnik as 'one small ball in the air', but actually the Americans worked feverishly to catch up. That December they launched a Vanguard rocket designed by Werner von Braun, a German rocket expert who had joined them at the end of the Second World War. All it could carry was a tiny, 1.8 kg satellite, scarcely big enough for a mouse let alone a dog. Worse still, right there, in front of the television cameras of the world, the rocket rose just 60 cm above the launch platform - and fizzled out. 'Phutnik', as the rocket was dubbed by the newspapers, was a disaster.

It wasn't until January that the Americans managed to launch their own satellite - a pathetic thing the size of a milk bottle.

BUT THAT IS A MILK BOTTLE!

Something would have to be done. The Americans founded *NASA* (National Aeronautics and Space Administration) in July 1958. They were determined to catch up.

SPACE TRAINING

Once both sides had managed to launch satellites into orbit, obviously the next thing was to launch a spaceman. Because neither side had any experience of sending men into space they had no idea what sort of person would be best for the job. The Americans toyed with asking danger-seekers such as sky divers or even bull fighters, but eventually both sides settled on airforce pilots.

Training was very tough. Astronauts and cosmonauts ◄ were spun, shaken, jolted, frozen, baked in special chambers and worked to exhaustion on treadmills. The Americans had a special plane which could imitate zero gravity by swooping suddenly from very high up. It became known as the 'vomit comet'.

 A *cosmonaut* is a Russian astronaut.

1961: *First man in space.* In April 1961, Vostok, the Soviet manned space module, was blasted into space by a giant ICBM from the Soviet launch pad in Kazakhstan in the southern USSR. Vostok hurtled through the emptiness of space then re-entered Earth's atmosphere like a flaming ball. At around 7,000 metres, the hatch blew open, the cosmonaut Yuri Gagarin was ejected from his seat and descended gently by parachute. Yuri was chosen to be the first man in space because, among other things, he was small enough not to get stuck in the hatch.

1964: *Three men in space.* The Americans were soon to launch their two-man Gemini missions, but the Soviets beat them to it by launching a three-man mission in October 1964, in a stripped-down Vostok module with no room for spacesuits or any kind of emergency equipment.

1965: *The first space walk.* For nine minutes in March 1965, all went well as cosmonaut Aleksey Leonov hung in empty space high above Siberia. Unfortunately his spacesuit then began to swell up and went rigid - the dreaded 'football-bladder' effect caused by motion stresses. Leonov couldn't bend to get back through the hatch of his space vehicle. After eight further minutes of desperate struggle, with his oxygen running low, he finally managed to reduce the pressure in his suit and to squeeze back to safety. To cap it all, he landed in a forest and had to light a fire to keep the wolves at bay.

1966: *Moon landing.* Once both sides had successfully launched men into space, the next step was to land someone on the Moon. The first soft landing on the Moon by an unmanned craft was by the Soviets in February 1966. Lunar IX sent back pictures of the surface.

1968: First men to escape from Earth's gravity and not just into orbit. Three American astronauts, Frank Borman, Jim Lovell and Bill Anders, blasted off from Cape Canaveral, the NASA launch base in Florida, in December 1968. As they left Earth's gravity they reached a maximum speed of 37,379 kph (23,226 mph), the fastest speed ever flown by humans to that date. They flew out to the Moon, swung round it and returned safely to Earth.

July 1969: First men on the Moon. Americans Buzz Aldrin and Neil Armstrong landed safely on the Moon and walked on its surface. They left behind them a medal commemorating fellow spacemen who had died during the space race, including Yuri Gagarin who had died recently in a plane crash - the Cold War wasn't totally cold.

WINNING FEATS

By being the first to land men on the Moon, the Americans won the space race. The technology which won it for them would have seemed quite incredible a mere twenty years earlier when the Cold War started.

The craft which took them from their space module to the surface of the Moon and back again could accelerate from 0 to 4,827 kph (0 to 3,000 mph) in just two minutes.

The only man-made noise louder than a Saturn rocket at take-off is that of a nuclear explosion. Apollo-Saturn rockets with boosters and spacecraft, the type used on the Moon missions, were the heaviest objects ever to fly as well as the noisiest. They were the most powerful machines ever built and they were the size of Second World War destroyers tipped on end (108 metres/360 ft). The building in which they were put together had a larger volume than any building ever built.

Sergei Pavlovich Korolev (1906-66)

Russian triumphs in the Space Race were largely due to one man: Sergei Korolev. Korolev was an engineer and rocket designer of genius. During Stalin's terror of the 1930s he'd been sent to a labour camp and worked for several months in a gold mine under terrible conditions which ruined his health. Later in a 'special' labour camp for scientists, he worked with the great aircraft designer Alexander Tupolev, whom a make of Russian aircraft is named after.

In 1958 Khrushchev asked Korolev to design Russia's first manned spacecraft. Korolev was responsible for Sputnik, for Gagarin's Vostok craft and for the first space walk among other things, as well as for the giant rockets which threw them into space.

During his last illness he was often too tired to climb the stairs to his flat at the end of a day's work and often spent the whole night on the steps. Finally, he was operated on by the Soviet Minister of Health himself, who was a doctor. Unfortunately there were complications and Korolev died of a haemorrhage (bleeding).

I SPY WITH MY LITTLE EYE

SECRET AGENTS AND OTHER GADGETS

SPIES IN THE SKY

One of the things that most annoyed the Americans at the start of the space race was the fact that Sputnik flew right over America four times. They didn't like the thought of communists peering down at them without permission. And quite right too - satellites were, and are, perfect for spying.

NOT SO LOWE

Actually, spying from the air is not a new development. Way back in 1861, at the start of the American Civil War, a Yankee balloonist named Thaddeus Lowe was arrested as a Union spy after drifting over South Carolina in high winds.

You too

Air photography is ideal for spotting the build-up of enemy troops or the placement of missiles. By comparing photographs taken a few days or weeks apart, experts can spot the tiny changes which mean trouble is afoot: lorries newly parked in a clearing perhaps, or a new road built at night.

The Americans led the way. The first U-2 spy plane (stands for Utility 2) was flown in 1955. The U-2 was halfway between a glider and a jet plane. It had very long wings and could soar huge distances at very high altitudes - way too high for Russian fighter planes. At 21 kilometres up (about 13 miles) the pilots had to wear pressure suits or their blood would have boiled and they would have exploded.

Early U-2s carried cameras which could pick out an object the size of a baseball at 21 kilometres (13 miles). President Eisenhower was shown a picture of himself playing golf taken from that height. He could see the golf ball.

THAT'S ME!

For five years American U-2s were able to sail above communist territory at will. It was U-2s which spotted the build-up of Russian missiles on Cuba at the start of the Cuban Missile Crisis. But life became a lot more dangerous for U-2 pilots by 1960 when a U-2 was shot down by improved Soviet anti-aircraft missiles over the USSR. The pilot, Gary Powers, survived to claim that it was all a misunderstanding, but his high-tech cameras and his suicide needle proved otherwise.

Later spy planes were even more amazing. The American SR-71 spy plane could fly at a height of 38 kilometres (23 miles) at 4,183 kph (2,600 mph). It could photograph 100,000 square miles of territory in an hour. Most missiles had trouble catching up with it.

SATELLITE SIGHTS

Satellites proved to be more useful than planes because, once up they stay up. A satellite in geo-stationary orbit can hang above the same patch of

---

Geo-stationary orbit means that an object circles the earth at the same speed as Earth itself is rotating, so it appears to stay in the same place.

earth for years, soaking up information from down below which it then beams back to its owner. By the early 1960s, American spy satellites had cameras which were powerful enough to  make out all the cars in Moscow's Red Square from many miles overhead.

Plans were afoot for a nuclear powered satellite radar dish which would have been the size of a football pitch - although as thin as kitchen foil.

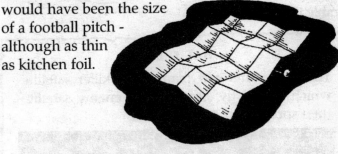

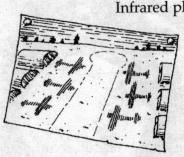

Infrared photographs taken from satellites could show the heat 'shadow' of planes on an airport runway hours after they had taken off.

SPACE INTERCEPT

A problem with satellites is that the other side may be able to tap into the stream of information which they send back to earth, often in the form of radio waves. It's not much use knowing what the enemy is up to if the enemy knows what you know.

It may even be possible for an enemy to tap into the stream of instructions which go the other way: from earth to the satellite - to take the satellite over in other words. The enemy may be able to make it roll and tumble out of control.

SAT SPLAT

The Americans had plans for a killer satellite which would fly alongside an enemy satellite then spray paint on its sensors.

LAND INTERCEPT

During the Cold War, both sides went to great lengths to intercept each other's secret information, not just in space but on earth as well.

American submarines tapped into Russian underwater cables.

The Americans tunnelled under Berlin in order to tap into Soviet land lines - until the scheme was given away by a British spy called George Blake who was a secret communist.

SPIES ON THE GROUND

There's a limit to what you can find out with a spy plane or a satellite. They can't tell you what the enemy are *planning*. Both sides in the Cold War used real human spies to get hold of secret enemy documents. In fact, there were so many spies that it was almost an industry. The Soviet Union had a special college for spies, the Andropov Institute. Students studied for six days a week for three years. During training they wore the clothes, smoked the cigarettes and learned the language of the country where they would do their spying. A tape recorder played news broadcasts and other radio programmes from the country twenty-four hours a day.

There were, and are, two kinds of spies: illegals and agents. An *illegal* is someone who goes to live in a foreign country and passes himself off as a citizen of that country while spying against it, as the students at the Andropov Institute were trained to do. An *agent* is someone who agrees to spy against his or her own country - a traitor in other words.

Usually Cold War illegals didn't do any actual spying. Their job was to recruit agents to do it for them. They were trained to watch out for likely agents and were specially interested in people whose work allowed them to see military secrets. There were several reasons why someone might become an agent:

Agents might actually believe in the cause they were spying for. Four of the very best Soviet agents were British students who became dedicated communists while at Cambridge University in the 1930s. Their names were Donald Maclean, Kim Philby, Anthony Blunt and Guy Burgess. They were known as the 'apostles'.

Some people became agents in order to make money - they sold their secrets in other words.

SO YOU COLLECT TOILETS, DO YOU?

Others were trapped or blackmailed into spying by an illegal who had found out something bad or embarrassing about them.

TRADE CRAFT

Spies led incredibly dangerous lives. If caught, they were treated as traitors and might be executed, as was the fate of the Rosenbergs, a married couple who betrayed American nuclear secrets to the Russians and were executed in Sing Sing prison, New York, in 1953.

The most dangerous time for any agent was when they had to make contact with their 'case officer', probably the illegal who recruited them. Usually this was either to be paid or to hand over secret information. Such contacts were very carefully set up.

The agent might leave a message in a 'dead letter box', which the case officer would pick up later. The dead letter box could be anything: a disused pipe, a crack in a gravestone, a hollow tree in the park. The case officer

would keep an eye open for signals telling him that a message was waiting. The signal might be a doll placed in the window of a house or a car parked in an unusual way. Such signals also served as warnings of danger or requests for meetings.

One agent used to leave top secret documents from his work in a hollow tree in Central Park, New York during his lunch hour. His Russian case officer would take them away, copy them quickly and then return them so that the agent could replace them without anybody knowing they'd been taken. Imagine the case officer's horror when he came to collect the documents and found Central Park full of pieces of paper marked 'Top Secret' blowing around in the wind. A squirrel had decided to make its nest in the hollow tree and it didn't need all that paper!

Luckily a friendly and unsuspecting policeman helped the Russian to pick them up!

Secrets could be hidden anywhere.

A small coin hollowed
to take microfilm.

A secret code written on 250 pages of
paper so thin that it could be rolled up
and kept in a hollowed-out pencil.

Assassins!

Spying was a dirty business. Department V of the
KGB, the Russian secret service (see page 83), kept a
list of leaders in every major country, due to be
murdered if war broke out. They had plans to flood
the London Underground and to scatter poison
capsules in the corridors of British government
ministries which would kill whoever trod on them.

WHERE ARE THE FLOOR CLEANERS THIS MORNING?

The KGB also developed an electrically
operated gun which would fit inside a
cigarette packet, and a spray gun
which fired a jet of poison gas. The
gas killed the victim in such a way
that it looked as if the victim had had
a heart attack.

DIRTY TRICKS

Secret assassins were useful because the Cold War had to be fought without fighting, at least not directly. Of course, at one extreme there were the major conflicts such as the Korean War (see page 38) and the Vietnam War (see page 42), where American soldiers fought local communists who were supplied by the Russians. But at the other extreme, both sides killed sneakily. Their targets tended to be foreign leaders who might be a danger to them.

The *CIA* (Central Intelligence Agency, the American secret service) supplied the guns which killed Dominican dictator Rafael Trujillo in 1961. His government was so unpopular that many Dominicans were starting to support communist rebels. The CIA probably also supplied parts of the bomb which killed a former Chilean ambassador in Washington.

The point was to make sure that friendly governments were in power wherever possible - and it didn't really matter how awful they were, provided they were friendly. Both sides were at it. Tyrants from Santiago to Seoul, in Africa, Asia and South America, were given guns by the truckload to help them hang onto power. Meanwhile, secret (and not so secret) convoys of guns were sent by the other side to any rebels who might be fighting against the tyrants. Always the Americans and the Russians helped opposing sides. It didn't seem to matter too much who they helped. Both sides in the Cold War worked on the age-old principle:

My enemy's enemy is my friend.

I SPY QUIZ

(Answers on page 123.)

1 **Why did U-2 pilots have to wear pressure suits?**

a To make them work hard
b To stop them exploding
c To stop their blood boiling

2 **What were killer satellites supposed to do?**

a Crash into enemy satellites
b Shoot missiles at enemy territory
c Spray paint at enemy satellites

3 **Who were the apostles?**

a A group of Cambridge students who became British spies
b A group of Cambridge students who became communist spies
c The followers of Jesus

4 **What did Department V of the KGB plan to do to British government ministries?**

a Kill all ministers with a poison spray gun
b Scatter poison capsules in the corridors
c Flood the basements with poisonous fluids

WALLED IN!

BEHIND THE IRON CURTAIN

DON'T WANNA GO HOME!

One of the worst things you could do with a Soviet spy was - to send him back to Russia! It was common practice for the two sides to swap captured spies. It saved the trouble of keeping them in prison. When Soviet spy Rudolf Abel was being taken to East Germany from America to be swapped with Gary Powers (see page 72) in 1962, he was closely watched by two American secret service men for the entire journey. They were worried that he might try to kill himself rather than go home!

The problem was that, having been turned into a giant prison camp by Lenin and Stalin, the USSR never really changed back again. No one could go in and no one could get out without permission. Those who did manage to escape to the west, or 'defect' as it was called, might find themselves kidnapped and forced home. This could happen to anyone. Stalin's daughter

Svetlana defected in 1966, but even she wasn't safe. A KGB (see below) strongman was sent to kidnap her, although luckily the plot failed.

All along the border between east and west the Soviets built watchtowers, razor wire fences, killing zones and dog runs to keep their people in. Most famous of these barriers was the Berlin Wall but it was far from being the only one. Those who wanted to escape had to tunnel their way out or dash for freedom as best they could. Many never made it.

KGB

The KGB (*Komitet Gosudarstvennoy Bezopasnosti* or 'Committee of State Security') ran the Russian border guards among other things. It was set up in 1954 after the death of Stalin and, believe it or not, it was a positive softy compared to what had gone before. Under Stalin's NKVD some *5 million people per year*

NKVD stood for 'People's Commissariat of Internal Affairs' in Russian.

83

had been kept in a vast network of forced labour camps (like prisons, but where everyone has to work very hard) known as the *Gulag* . Around 10% died of ill treatment in an average year. After Khrushchev came to power in 1953, millions of people were released.

The KGB was quite simply the largest secret service organisation the world has ever known. It ran the spies and the border guards and the secret police who kept everyone in line. At its peak it had 300,000 border guards, 400,000 security officers and countless informers in the USSR, as well as spies and other secret agents overseas.

TIME FOR A PARTY

One of the main differences between the KGB and Stalin's terrifying NKVD was that the KGB was firmly under the control of the *Communist Party*. So at least top communists were safe from arrest - which hadn't been the case before.

The *Communist Party of the Soviet Union* was the old Bolshevik Party (see page 18) grown up. On paper, 'Party' and government were meant to be two different things, but in practice the Party ruled. It was

Gulag stood for 'Corrective Labour Camps' in Russian.

a giant octopus which spread its tentacles into every nook and cranny of Soviet life. In every factory, on every farm, in every school there was a communist branch - over 390,000 such branches in the 1980s.

Because the Communist Party was communist, it didn't believe in letting private factories decide what to make. Everything had to be planned by the government. The planning was done by *Gosplan*, the State Planning Committee, and it was *hopeless*. One year there might be too many tractors and not enough trains. The next year it might be the other way around. There were *never* enough cars or anything else you might need for yourself. To get a car you might have to wait ten years even if you had the money. The shops in the USSR were normally half-empty. Long queues would form outside them as soon as something that people actually *wanted* went on sale.

And what a party!

Because the Communist Party was all-powerful, you had to be a member of it to get to the top. Millions of ambitious young Russians joined the *Komsomol*, the 'All-Union Leninist Communist League of Youth'. Most of them didn't care two hoots about communism.

The top was worth getting to. Communism is meant to be classless, but the Soviet Union developed a 'communist' ruling class quite early in its history. They were called the *nomenklatura* , the people who mattered. They were the top people of the communist world, the administrators, managers, university professors and politicians. They shopped in their own special luxury shops, they had special holiday cottages and went to special holiday resorts. They drove in luxury limousines. If they were lucky they travelled abroad - the biggest privilege of all.

AH, THE SUN, THE SAND, THE VODKA.

NOT A WORKER IN SIGHT.

EXCEPT THE WAITER!

Nomenklatura comes from the Latin *nomenclator*. A *nomenclator* was a slave who told his master or mistress the names of people so that the master or mistress didn't have to remember them.

After Leonid Brezhnev took over as leader from Nikita Khrushchev in 1964, the corruption and luxury lifestyle of the top people got completely out of hand. Brezhnev's own daughter Galina and her husband went in for diamond smuggling and currency speculation on a grand scale.

Some of the top people were extremely flashy. Victoria Mzhavanadze, wife of the communist boss of Georgia in the south of the USSR, used to give massive parties in her *seven* luxury villas. To help pay for them, she and her husband took a cut from the sale of cars stolen in Moscow. Their corrupt seventeen year rule was known as the 'Victorian Era'.

Brezhnev himself collected a *fleet* of cars. There was a joke about him: his mother visits him and sees the fleet of cars, the swimming pool, the yacht and the luxury holiday homes and he asks her what she thinks of it all. She replies:

I'm worried in case the Bolsheviks return.

Boredom!

Life in the Soviet Union wasn't all bad. Provided you didn't question things too much or make trouble for the *nomenklatura*, you were safe from cradle to grave. Everyone had a job (of sorts) and nobody worked very hard - there wasn't much point since they were very unlikely to *lose* their jobs. Everyone had somewhere to live as well, even if living conditions were crowded.

It was just all terribly dull. You couldn't buy a house and do it up, start a business or go abroad on holiday. People need colour and excitement in their lives as well as safety.

Secretly, many young people started to look to the west. They bought copies of smuggled western rock music. The copies were made from X-ray film because there wasn't any vinyl in the USSR.

Some young men dared to grow their hair long which was the fashion of the time and gave themselves names such as *shtatniki* - a group who claimed to love the United States - and *beatniki* who were Russian beatniks, a western youth cult of the early sixties.

Meanwhile the communist leadership grew older and older. Like many old people in the west they loathed long hair and rock music. In Cuba, Fidel Castro the grey-haired leader of the revolution spoke out against long hair in extremely long, boring speeches. Girls wearing fashionable miniskirts were sentenced to labour camps in the Cuban countryside.

THE GREYING OF THE BEARDS

Josef Stalin (1879-1953).
Took power in 1924 aged forty-one.
Nikita Khrushchev (1894-1971).
Took power in 1953 aged fifty-six.
Leonid Brezhnev (1906-82).
Took power in 1964 aged fifty-eight.
Yuri Andropov (1914-84).
Took power in 1983 aged sixty-nine.
Konstantin Chernenko (1911-85).
Took power in 1984 aged seventy-three.

YOU'RE MAD!

In communist-controlled countries, the communist party controlled all the newspapers and other media. People were desperate to find out more about the world than what the communist media told them, so independent news reports, articles and even books were photocopied or carbon copies were made. Such copies, called *samizdat* (self published) in Russia, were passed from hand to hand. Meanwhile, thousands, if not millions, tuned into the *BBC World Service* or *Voice of America*, radio services which were beamed into the Soviet Union in Russian by a western world still keen to win the battle of ideas.

Some very brave souls, such as Andrei Sakharov, a famous nuclear scientist, dared to speak out against communist oppression. Stalin would have shot such people or sent them to the Gulag, but the KGB had another way of doing things. *Dissidents*, as they became known, might be sacked from their jobs and they would definitely not be allowed to travel abroad, but they probably wouldn't be shot. If they were especially annoying they might be declared insane and sent to a mental hospital. This was a clever trick because it was like prison but without the need for a prison sentence - and if dissidents were officially mad, whatever they had to say about communism must be mad too.

RED CHINA 🦶

Things were far tougher in China in the sixties and seventies than they were almost anywhere else. China had become communist in 1949 but Russia and China quarrelled in 1962. In red China, even thinking could be dangerous. During the Chinese Cultural Revolution of 1966-69, owners of foreign books were made to crawl on their knees in shame. If you could speak a foreign language, that was enough to prove that you were a spy.

Loyalty to the Chinese communist leadership could be a matter of life or death. During the Cultural Revolution, some followers of Chairman Mao Tse-tung, the Chinese leader, used to dance a 'loyalty dance' every morning:

You put your hand to your head and then to your heart and you danced a jig - to show that your heart and your mind were filled with boundless love for the Chairman.

Compared to that sort of nonsense, Russian communists were positively normal.

🦶 Striking Welsh miners are said to have first raised the red flag, a sheet dipped in blood, in Merthyr Tydfil in the nineteenth century. Since then red has been the colour of socialists and communists.

CRAZY COMMIE QUIZ

(Answers on page 123.)

1 What was Gosplan?

a A plan to increase goose production in the Soviet Union

b A Soviet plan for the invasion of West Germany

c The Soviet planning authority

2 What were the nomenklatura?

a Slaves who were employed to remember people's names in Ancient Rome

b The top people of the Soviet Union

c The top people of Ancient Rome

3 What did beatniki look like?

a They had long hair and wore sandals

b They had short hair and wore suits

c They had long hair and wore suits

d They wore nothing but a strip of X-ray film around their middles

4 What did owners of foreign books have to do during the Chinese Cultural Revolution?

a Read them

b Crawl on their knees in shame

c Translate them into Chinese so that other people could read them too

WALLED OUT!

THE FREE WORLD - SO THEY THINK

MENACING REDS

As early as 1950, many people, especially in America, were very frightened of the 'Red Menace' as they called the communist threat. People thought there were 'commies' all over the place - 'reds under the bed' as the saying went.

American children could collect chewing gum cards headed: 'Fight the Red Menace'.

One classic American scare movie became very popular. It was called *I Was a Communist for the FBI* .

Four million copies of a comic were distributed to children by an American religious trust. The comic was called *Is This Tomorrow - America Under Communism*.

FBI stands for 'Federal Bureau of Investigation'. It deals with internal threats to United States' security.

The Monster

At its most extreme, American anti-communism was an ugly thing. Ugliest of all was Senator Joe McCarthy, a heavy-drinking, belching, swearing bully who led an anti-communist crusade from 1950-54. McCarthy was a liar through and through. He even pretended to limp from a war wound which he never had. He claimed that the American government was riddled with secret communist sympathisers and whipped up a storm of hatred against these supposed traitors. A typical McCarthy rally was attended by groups such as *We the Mothers Mobilise*, *Alert Council of America* and *Minute Women of America* all of whom spat hatred of 'reds'. He went on to form his own group: the *Loyal American Underground*. Nothing was ever proved, but many innocent people inside and outside the government lost their jobs because of him.

McCarthy's success was odd but a sign of the times, and the fear he created was real enough. President Truman said of him:

… nothing more contemptible has ever occurred in the long history of human spite and envy.

Money, money, money

America became very rich during the Cold War. Even during the Second World War a lot of American businessmen became extremely wealthy by supplying arms and other goods to the Allies . Britain meanwhile had borrowed money from America to help buy the arms. When it came to discussing how to repay the money, as the American representative at the discussions put it:

> *We loaded the British loan negotiations with all the traffic the market could bear.*

Meaning they squeezed as much money out of Britain as they could. Robert Boothby, a British politician, remarked that the terms of repayment were those 'usually reserved for a defeated enemy'. A poor reward for British courage. At the end of the war America held 46% of the world's gold reserves. This rose to 72% in 1949, three years later, in large part due to British loan repayments.

The *Allies* were the British, French, Americans and others. On the other side was the Axis which was basically Germany and her friends.

But then America woke up to the *Red Menace*. If America didn't start being nicer, the whole of Europe, including Britain, might go communist. That was when the Americans began to pour Marshall Aid into Europe (see page 33).

But *still* America got richer. It was the only great power to have survived the Second World War intact and its factories were ready to churn out whatever the world wanted to buy. The arms race with Russia simply fuelled the fire. American arms manufacturers grew fat by supplying arms to the American armed forces. The armed forces and the arms manufacturers were like cats lapping at a limitless bowl of cream. Armed forces bigwigs retired to work for arms manufacturers and top arms manufacturers advised the armed forces on what arms they should buy.

FAT CATS

THE FAT OF THE LAND

Life in the Soviet bloc stayed tough during the Cold War, but life in America and then in Europe got better and better. Before the Second World War only the rich had cars. By the 1950s, even quite ordinary Americans could afford the long, gas-guzzling monsters of the period, fitted out with fins, air-conditioning and lots and lots of chrome.

The children of the car-owners, born during or immediately after the Second World War, grew up in a brave new world of cars and money. They were called the 'baby-boom' generation because there were millions of them. They had more money than young people had ever had before and this gave them independence, even though their parents struggled to keep them under control. 'Teenagers' as a particular group were invented in the 1950s and a whole youth industry sprang up to give them what they wanted. To start with:

Rock and roll

Winkel-pickers (shoes with long, pointed toes)

Jive

America boomed along with the baby-boomers, and the 'free world' followed in her footsteps. Young American Cold War soldiers, stationed in Europe and Asia in case of communist invasion, brought all things American with them. Things which nowadays we take for granted:

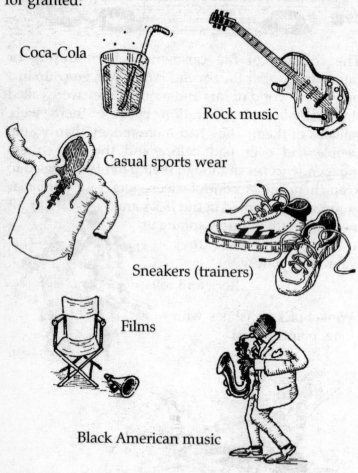

Coca-Cola

Rock music

Casual sports wear

Sneakers (trainers)

Films

Black American music

European baby-boomers didn't have as much money as American baby-boomers but many of them followed American pop culture just the same. It was hard not to, it oozed over the world like ketchup over a big, fat American hamburger. The way it spread was called 'cultural imperialism' and some people tried to stop it. The French National Assembly voted to:

> … prohibit the import, manufacture and sale of Coca-Cola in France, Algeria and the French colonial Empire.

Fat hope.

THE DOWN SIDE

Of course, as the Russians never tired of pointing out, things were far from perfect in the 'free world'. In America the black population was badly treated, especially in the south. How free is a nine-year-old black boy sentenced to fourteen years in prison for kissing a seven-year-old white girl, as happened in North Carolina in 1958? That's one thing that never happened in the USSR.

Understandably, American blacks became fed up. They wanted an equal share of the 'American dream'. At first they campaigned peacefully but black 'freedom marches' were sometimes broken up by police dogs and water cannon. In the mid-sixties, angry black people rioted in the streets of several American cities.

At the same time as young black Americans were rioting, a scratchy, grumbly mood spread among white baby-boomers in both America and Europe. This mood was fed by the Vietnam War which reached fever pitch in the mid-1960s. Thousands of young Americans fled to Europe and Canada so as not to have to fight in a far-away war which they didn't believe in.

Mass protests of students and others demanded that America get out of Vietnam. America was split down the middle about the war and anti-war protesters were spied on by the CIA  . There were similar protests in Europe. In France in 1968, students, rioting over poor conditions in the French universities, took over Paris. The French President Charles de Gaulle fled to Belgium before returning to ring Paris with tanks and take back control of the city. The Russians must have rubbed their hands as they looked on.

 CIA stands for 'Central Intelligence Agency'. The CIA is the central spying agency of the United States.

Peace, man!

This was the era of long-haired hippies. Their ideas seem a little simple-minded nowadays: nuclear weapons are awful, the Cold War is awful, capitalism is awful: since protest hasn't changed things, perhaps wishful thinking will do the trick. Hippies believed in 'Peace' with a capital 'P'. Peace would come if everybody wanted it to. Which was fair enough - except of course, not everybody *did* want it to.

And revolution, man

While the hippies chanted and played with their beads, many students became communists, although not Soviet communists. Since the Russians had long since betrayed the old communist ideal, the students chose new heroes such as the Cuban revolutionary, Che Guevarra, and the Chinese communist, Chairman Mao Tse-tung. Mao was an odd choice since he was as much of a brute as Stalin had been - but somehow his fans managed to ignore this.

REDS IN BED QUIZ

(Answers on page 123.)

1 What classic American scare movie was popular in the 1950s?

a I Was a Communist for the FBI
b I Was a Communist for the CIA
c I Was a Red Menace for the KGB

2 What did Joe McCarthy pretend to do?

a Hate communism
b Walk with a limp due to a war wound
c Drink heavily

3 What terms of repayment did the Americans impose on the British for their war loan?

a Harsh
b Mild
c Britain didn't have to repay the loan at all

4 What did the French National Assembly vote to do?

a Introduce a French brand of Coca-Cola into their colonial Empire
b Prohibit all sales of Coca-Cola in their territories
c Import extra quantities of Coca-Cola into France because it tastes so good

COLD WAR COUNTDOWN - PART 2

FINGERS OFF THE TRIGGER
- AND ON AGAIN

By 1975, NATO and the Warsaw Pact had been growling at each other like bears in a bear pit for over twenty years. But although they growled, they agreed to live and let live in the grudging spirit of *détente* (see page 44). This was made official in the *Helsinki Accords* of 1975, agreed in Helsinki the capital of Finland. It was at Helsinki that the west bit the bullet and finally accepted communist control of eastern Europe - thirty years after the end of the Second World War. It looked like *détente* was here to stay.

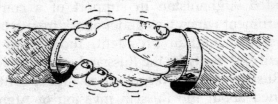

Then everything went wobbly.

FREEZING OVER AGAIN

1977: The USSR replaced some out-of-date missiles in eastern Europe with SS-20s. The SS-20 was a new and more accurate IRBM or *Intermediate Range Ballistic Missile*. 'Intermediate range' meant that it didn't have very far to travel. It could hit any target in western Europe in less than ten minutes from take off. By the time western defences spotted them, the west would have less than *two minutes* to react. Nuclear war was a hair trigger business at the best of times, but this was *seriously* hairy.

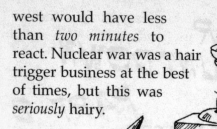

1979: NATO voted to place Cruise and Pershing missiles in Europe (including Britain) in response to the SS-20s. Cruise and Pershing were also intermediate range nuclear missiles. They could hit Moscow in less than ten minutes. Now both sides felt threatened.

1979: On Christmas day, Russian soldiers invaded Afghanistan in support of a communist government which was under attack from rebels. The communist Afghan president, thought to be too violent and nasty by the Russian leadership, was shot by Russian soldiers disguised as Afghans. Brezhnev worried about the Russian invasion of Afghanistan even as he agreed to it. He said:

> ...*we must not do this. It would only play into the hands of our enemies.*

It did.

1980: Ronald Reagan was elected President of the USA. Reagan thought *détente* was for sissies, especially after the Russians invaded Afghanistan. He called the Russian leadership the 'focus of all evil in the modern world' and planned for a huge American arms build-up. Together with British Prime Minister Margaret Thatcher, he led the west back on the Cold War warpath.

1981: The Russians were so frightened by Reagan that they started 'Project Ryan'. Ryan was huge - and a bit mad. KGB spies were instructed to count the number of lighted windows in NATO and western government buildings and the number of cars parked outside them. They were to look for signs of increased activity which might signal the start of war.

DO WE HAVE TO STAY HERE ALL NIGHT!

Early 1980s: It wasn't only Russians who were frightened by President Reagan and the new arms build-up. Many people in the west were frightened too. There were big demonstrations against cruise missiles. CND, the Campaign for Nuclear Disarmament, was revived. Women peace protesters camped outside the American missile base at Greenham Common in Berkshire where some of NATO's cruise missiles were to be placed.

PEACE NOW

1982: Solidarity, a non-communist Polish trades union, took advantage of Russia's troubles in Afghanistan to demand extra freedoms at home. 50,000 Polish workers went on strike against their communist government, but a tough communist general clamped down and imposed strict military rule. By doing so, General Jaruzelski probably saved his country from Russian invasion, but the west was horrified.

1984: The long-awaited Cruise missiles were at long last positioned at their European bases. Western peace protesters went ballistic, if that doesn't sound too confusing.

The freeze had turned into permafrost. It might have stayed that way for a very long time if it hadn't been for one man ...

ENTER GORBY

THE END IS NIGH

Mikhail Gorbachev became leader
of the USSR in 1985. Nobody was ready for it.

GORBY BOX

Mikhail Gorbachev was a clever man. He was once described as having 'a nice smile and teeth of steel'. He was born in 1931 into the nightmare of Stalin's rule. During his childhood one of his peasant grandfathers was sent to Siberia , the other was imprisoned as an 'enemy of the people'. His elder brother and three uncles were all killed fighting in the Second World War. Gorby had to be tough as well as clever just to stay alive.

Back in 1961, at his very first Communist Party conference, he voted to have Stalin's corpse removed from its place of honour beside Lenin in Red Square, Moscow. Till then, both bodies had been preserved with embalming fluids, a bit like Egyptian mummies.

 Many Russian political prisoners and criminals were exiled to Siberia in the frozen north.

A MAN IN A HURRY

Gorbachev hit the ground running. As soon as he came to power, things began to happen fast. Ideas and attitudes which had been frozen solid for thirty years went soggy almost overnight.

The USSR was ripe for change. For years it had festered under Brezhnev and other elderly leaders, and the dead hand of the communist *nomenklatura* was everywhere.

However, younger members of that same *nomenklatura* felt ashamed when they travelled abroad. They saw how much better life was in the west and felt that they had to lie to their western friends about life in Russia, which was still horribly grim. For a proud country like Russia it was hard to be left behind.

Gorbachev put himself at the head of young communist reformers who wanted to turn Russia into a comfortable, modern country. He hoped to be able to do this but also to keep the best parts of the old communist ideal which had been so tragically corrupted by Lenin and Stalin. He came armed with two things: a tongue which could talk the hind leg off a horse, and the words *glasnost* and *perestroika*.

Glasnost meant 'openness'. Books and other documents which had been strictly forbidden under the old leadership were printed in their thousands. At long last Russians were able to read the true story of their recent history, which didn't make for pretty reading.

Perestroika meant 'restructuring'. Gorbachev set out to rid the Communist Party and the country of all the hidebound, corrupt managers and administrators who were clogging up the works and stopping his reforms.

YOU'RE SACKED

It's a START

Gorbachev understood that the Cold War was based on fear and he set out to get rid of the fear so as to get

NO TESTS! WHATS GOING ON? rid of the war. He announced that the USSR was stopping all tests of nuclear bombs immediately and that they wouldn't wait for the Americans to do likewise. *That* took the wind out of Reagan's sails.

Reagan however was a man of surprises. Once he saw that Gorbachev was serious about ending the Cold War, Reagan was pleased to join him in the great task. The two leaders met in Geneva in October 1985 and agreed to work towards a *START*, a 'Strategic Arms Limitation Treaty'.

ZERO OPTION

For the next eleven months Gorbachev and Reagan wrote privately to each other. In letters which were sometimes handwritten, they discussed how they could end the nuclear terror for good.

It all came to a head when they met again at Reykjavik, the capital of Iceland, the following October (1986). At Reykjavik, Gorbachev and Reagan tore up the rule book. They agreed to create a nuclear-free world - the *Zero Option*. Nothing was going to stop them - not even their assistants, who on both sides were worried about the recklessness of their chiefs.

The assistants had to do as they were told. And they had a hard job to keep up: in corners of bedrooms, in bathrooms, even on toilet seats, they scrambled to jot down the right words for the treaties which would hopefully be signed later. The Americans borrowed carbon paper off the Russians because there wasn't even a photocopier.

THAW

The Zero Option never quite came off, but even so both sides agreed to massive arms reductions. The thaw had set in and thanks to Gorbachev there was no stopping it. When President Reagan visited Moscow in

May 1988 he was cheered as a hero by the crowds. And in December of that year Gorbachev gave a speech in the United Nations which opened the floodgates to still greater changes:

> ... to deny a nation freedom of choice ... is to upset the unstable balance ... Freedom of choice is a universal principle.

This meant that as far as Gorby was concerned, the countries which had suffered under Russian rule since the end of the Second World War were free to choose between communism and capitalism. A 'Year of Miracles' was about to happen.

MIRACLES

February 1989: Communists in the Hungarian parliament accept the need for free elections and a multi-party state.

May 1989: Hungarian troops tear down the barbed wire barrier between Hungary and Austria, leaving a gaping hole in the Iron Curtain.

June 1989: A free election is held in Poland. It's won by Solidarity (see page 106). Polish communists give up power voluntarily.

Summer 1989: Thousands of citizens of communist East Germany leave for capitalist West Germany. They pour through the back door - through the gap in the Iron Curtain made by Hungary.

October 1989: Gorbachev refuses to help the East German communists when they want to stop their people escaping to the west. He visits Berlin where the crowds chant 'Gorby, Gorby, help us!'.

November 1989: Huge crowds surge towards the Berlin Wall. Army and police do nothing to stop them. The people tear gaps in the Wall almost with their bare hands and surge into West Berlin. The East German government falls.

The fall of the Berlin Wall marked the end of the Cold War.

THE PARTY'S OVER

CLEANING UP THE MESS

PEANUTS

When the Cold War ended, Russia and the countries of eastern Europe woke up to find themselves in a terrible mess. After decades of communism, their factories were stinking and polluting, they had no money, they had no proper system of law, and die-hard communists still clung to power wherever they could.

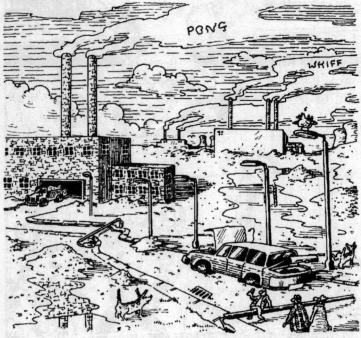

The countries of eastern Europe asked the west for help. However by 1989, America had a new president called George Bush. Bush was a lesser man than Ronald Reagan. What Bush and other western leaders gave their former enemies was peanuts compared with what was needed. One of the founders of Solidarity in Poland described Bush as:

Sleep-walking through history.

EXIT THE HERO

Eastern Europe had only suffered under communism since 1945, but Russia had suffered since 1917 (see page 18), so the mess in Russia was the worst mess of all. The Russian people wanted the mess sorted out, and fast. But that didn't happen. Gorbachev was a hero, but he was still a communist and he wasn't prepared to change Russia fast enough to meet the wishes of its people, and to put money in their pockets.

To be fair, probably no one could have sorted out the mess. But the Russians weren't in a mood for fairness. As it says in the Bible:

> *A prophet is not without honour save in his own country.*

So, like a mayfly which emerges into the light of day only to die before the day is over, Gorbachev failed to keep his job long enough to enjoy his miracle. It was on 19 August 1991, while Gorbachev was on holiday, that the 'Gang of Eight', a group of top generals, industrial managers and communist politicians, announced that they had seized power.

In fact at that point Gorby's day in the sun was almost over but not *quite*. During 1991, the old USSR, the Union of Soviet Socialist Republics, had broken up as one small country after another left it to strike out on its own. (Gorbachev stayed true to his principle of 'freedom of choice'.) Only the heartlands round Russia were left, but at least Russia now had its own Russian parliament lead by a Russian president, an ex-communist called Boris Yeltsin.

Inspired by Yeltsin, the people of Moscow surged onto the streets outside their parliament building to protest against the coup by the Gang of Eight. The last thing they wanted was a return to power of old-style

118

communists. The army refused to stop the protests and the coup of the Gang of Eight fizzled out like a damp squib. Just to make sure, the Russian parliament then passed a decree *banning* the Soviet communist party. Even a year earlier such a thing would have seemed impossible. On the streets outside, statues of Lenin and other communist leaders were toppled into the dust.

THE DEATH OF A DREAM

On 8 December 1991, eleven of the countries which had made up the old USSR voted to turn it into a 'Commonwealth of Independent States'. At that moment the USSR died. Two weeks later, on Christmas day, Gorbachev, the last leader of the Soviet Union was forced to leave his office in the Palace of the Kremlin in Moscow and the Hammer and Sickle, the flag of the Soviet Union was lowered for the last time. The old Russian flag of before the Bolshevik coup of 1917 was raised in its place.

The wheel had turned full circle.

DREAMS

WHERE WE STARTED

We started this book with a dream - well, a nightmare. Happily, any chance that the nightmare might come true is over for the time being. But the Cold War is still very recent history and many of the problems created by it are still with us, as are many new problems caused by its ending. Among other things, some nasty wars and squabbles have broken out in ex-communist countries.

On the up side, at least Russia is at last a democracy , although it's still a very tough place to live in. Let's hope things get better for them soon.

In a way the whole story of the Cold War is the story of a dream - the dream of communism. It was a

---

Democracy here means a country which chooses its government by voting for it.

beautiful dream but it went wrong because it didn't match up to reality, and there are few things more destructive than a dream like that.

One small lesson we can learn from the Cold War is to make sure that our own dreams do match up to reality. If we don't aim too low in life, but we don't aim too high either, like the communists did, things often work out fine.

ANSWERS TO QUIZ - OR
COULD YOU BE A
COLD WAR WARRIOR?

Score 10 points for each correct answer and
score other points as shown.

PAGE 25

*1-c. See page 13. Score minus 5 if you chose b.
Communists often use long complicated names but
not that long and complicated!*
2-b. It's got nothing to do with marks. See page 14.
3-a. See page 18. Minus 10 if you chose c.
*4-b. See page 23. But score 5 if you chose a, which
could also be true.*

PAGE 36

1-b. See page 26. Minus 5 for a. You must be daft.
2-c. See page 29.
*3-a. See page 32. Minus 5 for c - it's the wrong sort of
buck!*
*4-b. See pages 27-9. Minus 10 for a - you're not
concentrating.*

PAGE 53

1-c. See page 47.
*2-b. See page 48. Minus 5 for a or c. Your maths is
awful.*
*3-c. See page 51. Minus 5 for a. You're not
concentrating again.*
4-b. See page 48.

Page 81

1-b or c. See page 71. One thing leads to another.
Minus 5 for a.
2-c. See page 74.
3-b or c. See page 76/7 for b.
4-b. See page 79.

Page 92

1-c. See page 85.
2-b. A nomenclator was a type of Roman slave.
See page 86.
3-a. See page 88. Minus 5 for d, which is absurd.
4-b. See page 91.

Page 102

1-a. See page 93. Minus 5 for c.
*2-b. See page 94. He didn't pretend to drink
heavily and hate communism - he did!*
3-a. See page 95. Minus 5 for c.
4-b. See page 99.

Scores

*150-240. Excellent. You have a good
understanding of the issues and you would have
made an excellent recruit for either side!*
100-150. Not bad at all - for a beginner.
*50-100. Very mediocre. We suggest you read this
book again.*
0-50. Dreadful.
Less than 50. Worse than dreadful.

INDEX

first strike 58-9,61

Gagarin, Yuri 65,67,69
glasnost 109
Gorbachev, Mikhail 107-113,
   117-9
Gosplan 85
Greenham Common 105
Guevarra, Che 101
Gulag 84,90

Helsinki Accords 103
hippies 101
Hiroshima 31,32,38,49
Hungarian Uprising 40
hydrogen bombs – *see*
   nuclear bombs

ICBMs (Intercontinental
   Ballistic Missiles) *see*
   nuclear missiles
International Working Men's
   Association *see* First
   International
IRBMs (Intermediate Range
   Ballistic missiles) (*see* also
   nuclear missiles) 60,
   103-4,106
Iron Curtain 29,82,112,113

Jaruzelski, General Wojciech
   106

Kennedy, Jacqueline 43
Kennedy, John F. 5,6,8,43,
   44,54
KGB 79,83-4,90,105
Khrushchev, Nikita 6,8,38-9,
   43,54,69,84,87,89
Kim Il Sung 38

Komsomol 86
Korean War 38,80
Korolev, Sergei 69

Laika 63
League of the Just 13
Lenin, Vladimir Illyich 18,19,
   20,21,22,23,82,107,109,
   119
Leonov, Aleksey 66
Lovell, Jim 67
Lowe, Thaddeus 70

Maclean, Donald 77
MAD (Mutual Assured
   Destruction) 54,59,60
Manhattan Project 30
Mao Tse-tung 55,91,101
Marshall Aid 33,34,96
Marshall, General George
   Catlett 33
Marx, Karl 13-16
Marxism 14
McCarthy, Joe 45,94
McMahon, Senator 38
MIRVs (Multiple
   Independently-Targetable
   Re-entry Vehicles) *see*
   nuclear missiles
Mzhavanadze, Victoria 87

Nagasaki 31,32,49
Nagy, Imre 40
NASA (National Aeronautics
   and Space Administration)
   64,67
NATO (North Atlantic Treaty
   Organisation) 37,40,47,
   103,104,105
Nehru, Jawaharlal 55

NOW READ ON

If you want to know more about the Cold War, see if your local library or bookshop has either of these books.

SPY (EYEWITNESS GUDES SERIES)
By Richard Platt (Dorling Kindersley 1996). Spying was a major industry during the Cold War. This book is packed with information about spying from the earliest times. It gives all the background you could possibly need (if you're not a professional spy). It has excellent photographs of such tools of the spy's trade as microcameras, hidden weapons and code machines.

LEADERS OF THE RUSSIAN REVOLUTION
By Fred Newman (Wayland Publishing Ltd. 1981). The Russian Revolution happened before the Cold War proper, but it helps to explain how the War started. This book gives a good account of the drama of those days through descriptions of the communist leaders.

ABOUT THE AUTHOR

Bob Fowke is a well-known author of children's information books. Writing under various pen names and with various friends and colleagues, he has created many unusual and entertaining works on all manner of subjects.

There's always more to his books than meets the eye - look at all the entries in the index of this one!

3 8002 00936 7097

What They Don't Tell You About...
ORDER FORM

0 340 71330 5	ART	£3.99
0 340 63622 X	QUEEN VICTORIA	£3.99
0 340 63621 1	HENRY VIII	£3.99
0 340 69349 5	LIVING THINGS	£3.99
0 340 67093 2	SHAKESPEARE	£3.99
0 340 69350 9	STORY OF SCIENCE	£3.99
0 340 65614 X	ANCIENT EGYPTIANS	£3.99
0 340 65613 1	ELIZABETH I	£3.99
0 340 68611 1	VIKINGS	£3.99
0 340 68612 X	WORLD WAR II	£3.99
0 340 70922 7	ROMANS	£3.99
0 340 70921 9	ANGLO SAXONS	£3.99
0 340 71329 1	PLANET EARTH	£3.99
0 340 71328 3	ANCIENT GREEKS	£3.99
0 340 68995 1	STORY OF MUSIC	£3.99
0 340 73611 9	OLYMPICS	£3.99

All Hodder Children's books are available at your local bookshop or newsagent, or can be ordered direct from the publisher. Just write to the address below. Prices and availability subject to change without notice.

Hodder Children's Books, Cash Sales Department, Bookpoint, 39 Milton Park, Abingdon, Oxon, OX14 4TD, UK.
Email address: orders@bookpoint.co.uk

Please enclose a cheque or postal order made payable to Bookpoint Ltd to the value of the cover price and allow the following for postage and packing:
UK & BFPO - £1.00 for the first book, 50p for the second book, and 30p for each additional book ordered, up to a maximum charge of £3.00.
OVERSEAS & EIRE - £2.00 for the first book, £1.00 for the second book, and 50p for each additional book.

If you have a credit card you may order by telephone - (01235) 400414 (lines open 9 am - 6 pm, Monday to Saturday; 24 hour message answering service). Alternatively you can send a fax on 01235 400454.